Enhancing Your Higher Education Presidency:

Fifteen Lessons on Leadership

Carolina,
All the best
in your own leadership
journey!
Elizabeth
Sept/20

Enhancing Your Higher Education Presidency:

Fifteen Lessons on Leadership

M. Elizabeth Cannon

Copyright © 2020 by M. Elizabeth Cannon

All Rights Reserved. No part of this publication may be reproduced, stored in a retrieval system, or transmitted, in any form or in any means—by electronic, mechanical, photocopying, recording or otherwise—without prior written permission.

Published by RENSAR Publishing

Edited by Margaret Chandler

Cover design by Patrick Brooks

ISBN: 978-1-7772835-0-6

Contents

Acknowledgments

The very nature of the academic environment, with its numerous stakeholders and complex structures, allows for leadership roles that are both exciting and daunting. This is particularly true for presidents of higher education institutions who are leading during unparalleled times of change. I would like to thank the many colleagues with whom I have worked for their inspiration, mentorship, support, and enlightening discussions during my own leadership journey. I would also like to thank the numerous family members, friends, and colleagues who provided thoughtful feedback on this book and on leadership in general. This includes Susan Belcher, Paul Davidson, Vania Grandi, Kevin Gregor, Pari Johnston, Nuvyn Peters, and Baljit Singh.

M. Elizabeth Cannon

Higher Education Leadership: Setting the Stage

THERE ARE TENS OF THOUSANDS of higher education institutions worldwide. Some are small and serve a regional footprint or have a particular focus; others are large with comprehensive program offerings and a global reach. And there are many in between. The overarching commonality among these institutions is their roles in preparing graduates to succeed and lead in a changing world and to be at the forefront of discovery, creativity, and innovation. The pace of change within the higher education sector is accelerating because of the many disruptions ranging from technology-enabled teaching and learning to increased accountabilities from funders and the public. There is also the expectation that institutions play a stronger role in community development and sustainability.

Given the increasing focus on the role of academic institutions to help shape healthy, equitable, and economically diverse communities globally, strong leadership is paramount. It is a privilege to serve as president of a higher education institution because the mission is important and the impact far reaching. Over time, however, expectations have changed significantly such that leaders must be increasingly resilient, nuanced, and effective to both recognize and capture opportunities, as well as to identify and mitigate risk.

Higher education institutions are inherently complex environments with multiple stakeholders and diverse views that are expressed openly and frequently. This is part of what makes them unique. The "organized chaos" fuels critical debate and creativity, ultimately shaping new ideas that may be translated and mobilized into new policies, processes, or products. Higher education institutional structures are relatively flat and, combined with academic freedom, can lead to individual behaviours or institutional cultures that aren't mirrored in other organizations. Effective leadership under these circumstances can be formidable. It is no wonder that many academics gladly defer to others to take up the gauntlet.

Role of the President

Leadership is a term broadly used to encapsulate the qualities expected of those who take on significant positions within organizations. It encompasses the characteristics one expects of a leader, such as integrity, confidence, and the ability to delegate. These characteristics help define a style of interaction and management as well as a personal approach to people, problems, and opportunities. Leadership also refers to deliverables that are expected including a vision, high-performance team, strong organizational culture—and ultimately—results. Someone who is seen as a great person but cannot deliver results will not fulfill their role as an effective leader. Leaving the organization in a tangibly better place than it was found is often a basic benchmark of effective leadership. Although this sounds straightforward, the steps to bridge strong leadership characteristics to increased organizational performance can be complex and elusive. Indeed, if it were easy, higher education institutions and their leaders would not have the challenges that regularly occur.

A higher education president sits between a CEO and an elected politician. On the one hand, academic institutions have large budgets and many employees with the usual needs for strategy, governance, risk management, and infrastructure. They need to be efficiently managed like they would in the private sector but without the same "bottom line." On the other hand, the multitude of stakeholders on and off campus necessitates sophisticated interpersonal skills to develop and nurture a broad range of relationships on behalf of the institution—this is the political nature of a presidency. Only when these two hands work together, will the president and the institution be fully successful.

During my academic career, I have had the opportunity to interact with exceptional academic leaders who exemplified and modelled the attributes that inspired me on my leadership journey. Similarly, I have witnessed presidents who struggled to find their voice and be effective on behalf of their institutions. I often reflect on what makes the difference. I suspect that part of the answer is that some people are better suited for leadership than others. However, I also strongly believe that leadership can be nurtured and strengthened through commitment and hard work.

Purpose

In this book, I share the lessons learned throughout my tenure as president of a large, research-intensive, Canadian university. The hope is to provide some practical advice to newly appointed presidents or others thinking about taking on such positions. Although the lessons are drawn from my own experiences and observations, they are not unique and will overlap with many who have been presidents before me. This book may also help higher education governing boards or presidential search committees better understand the president's role.

Great leaders make it look easy. They appear relaxed, decisive, and confident. It is like watching a professional athlete or musician at the top of their game. They are awe-inspiring in their performance, but because of their intense training over many years, a full appreciation of their talent and preparation is often missed by the layperson. I believe leadership is similar, including academic leadership, and this book provides some tools that support training and preparation. These tools will not necessarily make the job easier, but they will hopefully shed some light on the realities of the role and how to navigate the terrain more effectively.

The book contains 15 leadership lessons. Each lesson provides insight into a different slice of the leadership circle. In aggregate, these lessons provide a foundation that will support your leadership journey, which will constantly evolve throughout your experiences, both the good and the bad. At the end of this journey, you want to feel that you have made a difference and left your institution in a better place than you found it.

Lesson No. 1

Get to know yourself.

"Who you are, what your values are, what you stand for . . . They are your anchor, your north star. You won't find them in a book. You'll find them in your soul."

~Anne M. Mulcahy

A PRESIDENT'S IMPACT ON THEIR INSTITUTION can be profound. Their personal integrity, energy, ambition, communication skills, and support for accountability and transparency impact whom they recruit to their team, the level of support garnered from the community, and their ability to move their institution toward its strategic goals.

Being an effective higher education president starts with knowing yourself. Understanding your strengths and weaknesses and being realistic as to how these will affect your role is critical. This understanding will determine how you structure your office, the composition of your executive team, and what support systems you need to carry out your responsibilities.

All of the experiences you had before assuming a presidency give you insight as to what works for you to be successful. However, the role of president is more complex and exposed than other roles within the organization, and more so than most outside the academy. This means that weaknesses may be magnified and strengths harder to leverage on the presidential stage. A president operates in a public sphere with the potential for significant criticism and little praise. The only certainty is that not all stakeholders will be happy in the best of times, so having a thick skin and not taking criticism personally is important.

Being intentional with your leadership style will serve both you and your institution. Asking yourself "What do I want to be known for?" and "What do I want my reputation to be?" allows for the explicit identification of your aspirations and the expectations you have of yourself. Taking an honest inventory of your current leadership effectiveness gives you a realistic view of what skills, behaviours, and qualities you need to highlight or enhance to meet these aspirations and expectations.

A higher education presidency is a service role to your institution and its people, so being comfortable showing empathy, humility, and in some cases, vulnerability allows you to be authentic and approachable. Gaining an understanding of dimensions such as your comfort with conflict, sense of urgency, thinking processes, and personal motivations gives you perspective on how you approach people and issues. You will find this particularly important during times of stress when these dimensions are amplified. In short, you need to know what makes you tick.

One way leaders gain insight about their leadership and management style is to work with professional leadership coaches using various tools to assess their personality or create management or leadership profiles. There are many tools available, such as self-report questionnaires that can be compared to the general population or to executive leaders specifically. Often, a president will have a professional coach use these tools across the entire executive team so individual profiles can be shared and used to better understand and enhance team dynamics as well as build trust.

There is no one right leadership profile for a higher education president. The key is to understand your style and be transparent about areas where you may need support from others. This can be done by sharing your leadership and management profile with your executive team and board chair since they can complement and balance your strengths and weaknesses. For example, if you are an introvert and are uncomfortable with constant community engagement, using members of your team or higher education staff to accompany you to events and meetings may make the role more enjoyable.

Being personally and organizationally aware are critical aspects of effective leadership and this means being open to feedback. Most boards will perform an annual 360 degree evaluation whereby direct reports and members of the campus community, along with board and community members, will be asked for feedback on a president's leadership and management skills and competencies. This information is consolidated to provide a president with an assessment of their effectiveness and areas for development. Informal mechanisms should also be used, such as asking for feedback from your team members or from trusted community members who can provide feedback and advice in a safe environment.

The key is to earnestly digest the feedback with a goal to improve by constructing a development plan for the following year. Being surprised by constructive criticism may mean that you are not interpreting signals accurately from your team, the board, or other stakeholders. Getting feedback early in your tenure as president is also wise so you can address any concerns before they are entrenched.

Some presidents have difficulty understanding that what worked for them in previous roles will not work as president. Therefore, being able to pivot your leadership and management style without being defensive is essential. This entails being aware and realistic about your leadership and management capabilities and committed to ongoing improvement. This attitude may have the most significant impact on your tenure as a higher education president.

***

Key Takeaways from Lesson No. 1

Get to know yourself.

- Be intentional with your leadership style by asking yourself "What do I want to be known for?" and "What do I want my reputation to be?"
- Take an honest inventory of your current leadership effectiveness to give you a realistic view of what skills, behaviours, and qualities you need to highlight or enhance.
- Share your leadership and management profile with your executive team and board chair so they can complement and balance your strengths and weaknesses.
- Be open to formal and informal feedback to understand areas of effectiveness and areas for development, with a commitment to ongoing improvement.

Lesson No. 2

Use your time wisely.

"It is not enough to be busy . . . The question is: what are we busy about?"
~Henry David Thoreau

ONE OF THE FIRST OBSERVATIONS NEW PRESIDENTS make is how busy they are. And it's true the pace can be exhausting. Your office team may have your best intentions at heart by wanting you to meet key constituents—politicians, donors, student leaders, and alumni—early on. But this can quickly take its toll on the energy and time needed to build strong relationships with your executive team and board, let alone think about where you want to take the institution during your presidency.

What makes your job different from every other one on campus is the sheer breadth of issues and people you deal with. Your days are tightly scheduled leaving little flexible time, and the meetings within any given day can consist of managing reputational issues, strategizing about major donor opportunities, and interfacing with internal and external stakeholders to build relationships or promote your institution.

If you are not careful, the schedule will manage you rather than you managing the schedule. A presidency is not a 9 to 5 job, and your days, from early morning to late in the evening, can be easily filled because there is no shortage of tasks to complete and people to meet. Rather than being swept along, you need to be intentional so that the expectations of yourself and those around you are managed. This can be done by spending your time and energy on where *you* create value.

Focusing your time on the right activities starts with asking the question: "What can I do that no one else can?" As president, there are tasks and initiatives that can only be done or led by you. And these will evolve over time. In a president's first year, the focus might be on building a team, leading the development of an institutional strategy, strengthening governance practices, or getting the institution's financial house in order. In following years, it might be leading a fundraising campaign or launching a process to enhance the institution's culture. Some things on the list in the first year now require less of the president's time or are delegated to a team member.

Three recommended practices for best managing and allocating your time are the development of an annual performance plan aligned with the institutional strategic plan, a rigorous process for managing your schedule, and a disciplined approach to making commitments.

Developing a performance plan, which is a framework of goals, actions, and metrics that encapsulates your expected deliverables and results for the year ahead, is the first practice. As president, you need to drive the creation of your performance plan and those of your team. This level of clarity and accountability may not exist within your organization, and if not, it is your job to coach the team as you develop the plan. This may be challenging and stressful for some members since a solid performance plan requires both an understanding of purpose and action. If done well, the executive team will be better aligned with stronger trust and understanding around the table.

The actions and metrics of the performance plan should be clear and measurable. Performance plans are developed by the president in consultation with the board (and particularly the board chair) and provide an accountability structure to assess the president's progress and performance at year-end. Having a well-formulated performance plan sets expectations for the president and creates transparency for the board on where efforts will be focused. If goals and actions are not part of the performance plan, they are either not of high importance, not linked to the strategic plan, or will not be accomplished during the year ahead. Effectively, the plan determines what will be done and what won't. A president's performance plan should also link to their executive team's work and should flow down to their office staff. For example, if one of the actions to support a fundraising goal is to meet with 75 donors during the year, your scheduler should also have this as an objective so that expectations are aligned.

The second practice for managing time is to determine how much you actually have available and use it strategically. There are a surprising number of fixed commitments in a president's schedule that are driven by an institution's annual calendar, including convocations, specific recognition events, board and academic senate meetings (and some of their committees), and alumni weekends. These events can consume significant blocks of time and the remainder, although theoretically discretionary, needs to be carefully considered and strategically aligned. Your office should be adept at determining the strategic importance of meeting requests and opportunities so you can focus on driving the institution forward.

Establishing a schedule of whom you need to meet with, and at what frequency, lets your office organize your schedule for the year and protects you from undue chaos. Weekly meetings with your team, weekly or bi-weekly meetings with individual team members, and monthly meetings with the board chair, set a pace for you and those around you. Having blocks of time reserved to meet with students, donors, government leaders, and other stakeholders on and off campus ensures that this is not sacrificed by competing demands. In addition, many presidents are on the road for at least 25 percent of the time, so time away from home base needs to be productive. Each trip should have a strategic purpose, whether it is to network with relevant associations, advocate for government support, or develop long-term relationships with other institutions around the world. This focus also lets you balance your "internal" work with your "external" activities to make sure they are calibrated appropriately.

The third practice for managing your time is to be careful about commitments. As a higher education president, especially after a year or two, you will have many requests to sit on important committees, boards, and panels, with some being far away from home base. Each one needs to be considered for its value first and foremost to your institution, and second, to you personally. A rule of thumb is to never say "yes" when first asked. Take some time to think about the request and weigh its importance relative to your other commitments and your institution's goals. Providing regional, national, or international leadership is a vital role for a president; however, it is better to do a few things well than many things poorly. No one will think less of you if you decline because you don't feel that you can give the necessary time and effort to get the job done well.

And finally, don't complain that you are busy. Everyone is busy these days: the only difference is *how* people spend their time. Remember that being a higher education president is a privilege, and stakeholders look to you as a role model. Your ability to navigate myriad topics and commitments is part of the job, and being able to do this with a high level of energy and professionalism reflects well on you and your institution.

***

Key Takeaways from Lesson No. 2

Use your time wisely.

- Spend your time and energy on where *you* create value by asking the question "What can I do that no one else can?"
- Develop an annual performance plan tied to the institutional strategy with actions and metrics that are clear and measurable.
- Manage your schedule by differentiating between fixed commitments and strategic work to balance and calibrate "internal" and "external" activities.
- Practise a disciplined approach to making commitments to important committees, boards, and panels by considering their value to your institution and to you personally.

Lesson No. 3

Have a strategy and stick to it.

"Someone is sitting in the shade today because someone planted a tree a long time ago."

~Warren Buffett

HIGHER EDUCATION PRESIDENTS ARE OFTEN ASKED what their vision is for their institution. Stakeholders want a succinct and bold response that will elevate the institution's impact and reputation. Your ability to form and articulate such a vision will have a direct relationship to the attraction of new resources, the ability to build a strong team, and the recruitment of high-quality faculty, staff, and students. In short, vision matters.

A president's role in developing and articulating a vision for their organization cannot be overstated. Being able to sense—and challenge—their institution's ambition through a vision in order to increase its impact on stakeholders and the community has long-term impacts. Using creativity and foresight, a president must seek and understand multiple perspectives and voices from inside and outside their institution to inform and support a distinctive vision.

A vision must be encapsulated in a strategic plan so that it can be shared, put into action, and measured for progress. Effective leaders understand their primary role is to lead and steward strategy development and implementation. A president's ability to convene stakeholders, establish guiding principles for meaningful dialogue and engagement, and lead the enhancement of the institution's culture, all combine to support the development of a compelling strategy.

A strategic plan provides a mandate to the president throughout their leadership tenure, and its impact will be used to assess their performance by their board and stakeholders. It is also a shock absorber for disruptions since it is formulated on an evaluation of external trends and internal capacity such that course corrections can be made without losing sight of strategic goals. The process of developing a strategy takes significant time and resources as well as intellectual and emotional energy. If done well, the final result will be a dynamic vision that supports strategic goals that unify the campus.

A strategic plan provides a platform for decision making and resource allocation. It creates a framework to establish priorities for new initiatives, expanded programs, and increased investment in specific areas of focus. It is also about being able to say "no." The power of a strategic plan is that it supports leaders in making some choices and not others that are supported by a broadly endorsed and transparent strategy. It should underpin everything that is done within the institution.

Higher education institutions are some of the oldest institutions in society. With large infrastructure footprints, tenured faculty members, and unique governance systems, they often appear bureaucratic and hard to change. Investments—in people and facilities in particular—instinctively move an institution along a path that may be relatively fixed for a long period of time. This is why strategic plans need to be carefully created and implemented.

Most higher education strategic plans are for a five-year period. This means that a president will normally lead the development or review of one or two strategic plans over their leadership term. Given that strategic plans have long-term impacts, the five-year planning window is debated by some as being too short. The best strategic plans balance a long-term time frame with a sense of urgency. Even though a strategy may have a five-year span, its perspective should be 20 to 30 years with each successive strategic plan moving the institution along the path of achieving its vision. In this way, stakeholders can digest and understand what needs to be done in the near to medium term to ultimately achieve the long-term goals. If this is not the case, stakeholders will not have a sense of urgency and may disconnect from the strategy altogether.

The role of the president is to continually have their eye on the horizon while leading with a sense of purpose, urgency, and action. This requires a high level of consistency and discipline and often the commitment of successive presidents to the institution's long-term vision and goals.

***

Key Takeaways from Lesson No. 3
Have a strategy and stick to it.

- Challenge your institution's ambition and articulate a succinct and bold vision to increase its impact on stakeholders and the community.
- Use your strategic plan as a platform for decision making and resource allocation to establish new initiatives and programs and increased investment in specific areas of focus.
- Balance a long-term time frame with a sense of urgency so stakeholders understand what needs to be done in the near term to achieve the institution's long-term goals.
- Continually have your eye on the horizon while leading with a sense of purpose, urgency, and action.

Lesson No. 4

Translate strategy to action.

"Vision without execution is hallucination."

~Thomas Edison

HAVING A VISION WILL INSPIRE AND EXCITE your community both on and off campus. This excitement will quickly wane, however, if stakeholders perceive that the vision is only words and not actions. And actions without coherency will appear ad hoc and confusing unless they are clearly tied to a strategy. This is why vision must be translated to strategy that is then mapped to action.

The completion and approval of a strategic plan takes significant effort in terms of environmental scanning, consultation, iteration, and strategic goal development. Within the higher education sector, the process is as important as the final result since it will usually define the level of endorsement and commitment by stakeholders, particularly faculty members. It can be fraught with tension that is driven by internal politics, agendas—hidden or not—and the need to balance aspirational thinking with pragmatism to arrive at a strategy that will impact or transform the institution.

Once a new strategic plan is approved and launched, it positions the institution at a new starting line. The clock then starts ticking on how the strategy will have impact. Stakeholders will ask, "What will be different?" or "How will this affect my unit or faculty?" or "What can I do to contribute?" Answers to these questions will often determine if stakeholders will stay engaged in the strategy and its implementation or not.

An assumption often made by presidents is that once the strategy is in place, the heavy lifting is done and their team will organically start implementation. Some will also assume that stakeholders throughout the organization will naturally link the development of new programs, initiatives, or fundraising priorities to the strategy. These assumptions can lead to confusion and a lack of cohesion resulting in poor understanding and execution of the strategy or an outright failed strategy.

The translation of vision to strategy and strategy to action is accomplished by establishing priorities and key accountabilities. This is done through clear delegation, cross team and organizational communication, disciplined decision making, and the management of pace. It is the president's role to ensure that all these elements are in place.

The development of an operational plan that contains priorities, objectives, and timelines creates the roadmap to deliver the strategy over its lifespan. Key Performance Indicators (KPIs) are needed to measure year-over-year progress and to benchmark against peers to tangibly demonstrate impact to stakeholders.

The pace, or in other words "what gets done when," can be managed through a structured performance planning process for each executive team member and their portfolio. These plans need to be mapped to the annual business plan, which lays out what will be done each year in support of a typical five-year operational plan and strategy. A disciplined approach to action and implementation and recognizing that everything cannot be accomplished in one year will avoid chaos and burnout.

If all of these elements are implemented by the president, a line-of-sight between strategy, actions, and impact will be achieved. This is critical in the management of time, resources, and institutional capacity for change.

***

Key Takeaways from Lesson No. 4

Translate strategy to action.

- Translate vision to strategy and action by establishing priorities and key accountabilities through communication, clear delegation, and disciplined decision making.
- Develop an operational plan containing priorities, objectives, timelines, and KPIs as a roadmap for delivering and measuring the strategy's progress.
- Manage pace and avoid chaos and burnout through structured performance plans for each executive team member and their portfolio.
- Create a line-of-sight between strategy, actions, and impact to manage time, resources, and institutional capacity for change.

Lesson No. 5

Simplify complexity.

"If you can't explain it simply, you don't understand it well enough."
~Albert Einstein

HIGHER EDUCATION INSTITUTIONS are complex ecosystems with numerous stakeholders, disciplines, issues, and structures. The nature of an academic institution means that faculty (and in some cases staff) can operate relatively independently or in a silo with others without raising their heads to engage in institution-wide issues or dialogue.

To fully understand the various actors and politics of an institution will take time and effort, and being able to navigate this complexity is an important skill. This is potentially perilous for someone recruited externally who must come to terms with an unfamiliar institutional culture consisting of different traditions, norms, or behaviours. Taking time to understand an institution's culture is one of the first jobs of a new higher education president.

Against the backdrop of this highly complex environment, sometimes referred to as "organized chaos," it is the president's role to bring clarity. That is what simplifying complexity is all about. It encompasses clarity of message, intent, and action with the goal of aligning stakeholders with the vision and strategic plan. The challenge for presidents is the breadth and diversity of constituents and audiences that need to hear and understand where the institution is today, where it is headed, and what needs to be done to get there. Confusion will be the unfortunate result if stakeholders think that a president's message, intent, and actions are not cohesive.

There are three ways that you can simplify complexity. The first way is to prioritize. Focus on doing a few things well rather than many things poorly. Having a handful of key priorities that you focus on and regularly speak about leads to consistency. The saying "what interests my boss fascinates me" is very true. As the leader, where you focus your time and energy will automatically bring a level of focus to those around you and in your organization. In other words, being vocal and passionate about your priorities and those of the institution brings clarity to others.

The second way to simplify complexity is to be relevant. One of the most interesting aspects of being a higher education president is the diversity of people with whom you interact. On campus, there are faculty, staff, students, and board members, while off campus there are alumni, donors, government officials, and community leaders. Each of these stakeholders has an interest in your institution; however, what they may be specifically interested in will differ. As president, you must tailor your message to each audience by putting yourself in their shoes while remaining consistent between audiences. Getting the message right by understanding context creates relevancy for your audience, which is the goal. This may entail focusing on only a few ideas or developing a narrative with examples pertinent to the specific audience.

A third way to simplify complexity is to create a virtuous cycle where action leads to impact, which in turn creates value. The president must be able to animate how work being done in support of the institution's strategy leads to positive impacts, and they must provide tangible exemplars of success. Understanding the motivating values and interests of various stakeholders allows a president to be nimble and relevant to each one. This creates a strong and coherent narrative of the strategy in action. Showcasing to stakeholders how a strategy, which may seem illusive to some, leads to specific decisions, pro or investments builds momentum and support. This will look dil when engaging with students versus corporate leaders; however, maintain the support of diverse stakeholders is important.

***

Key Takeaways from Lesson No. 5

Simplify complexity.

- Simplify complexity through clarity of message, intent, and action to align stakeholders with the vision and strategic plan.
- Be vocal and passionate about a few select priorities to bring a level of consistency and focus to those around you and in your organization.
- Remain relevant by tailoring your message to each stakeholder by putting yourself in their shoes while being consistent between audiences.
- Construct a virtuous cycle by animating how work being done in support of the strategy leads to positive impacts and creates value.

Lesson No. 6

Don't fall into the hero complex.

"Leadership is about making others better as a result of your presence and making sure that impact lasts in your absence."

~Sheryl Sandberg

UNFORTUNATELY, ACADEMIC INSTITUTIONS often reward individual performance through incentivizing strong teaching, independent research, and service activities within the institution or community. Although the lone scholar model is being challenged through team research grants, partnerships within and among institutions, and evolving performance assessment systems, many academics generally operate quite independently with loose connections within their department, faculty, or discipline. Their team usually consists of their graduate students and other scholars in their research group, but the accountability for performance generally falls on their shoulders alone.

Once an academic is appointed to an administrative position, the concept of team changes. Support staff and other academic leaders become part of the equation, and the need to develop relationships with others to perform work increases. Many tasks and initiatives require expertise from numerous people, and this collective expertise must be woven together to achieve the desired results.

For a higher education president, the concept of team is further amplified. As the saying goes, "You will be judged by the company you keep," so building a strong team that is aligned to your—and the institution's—vision is crucial. No matter how much energy you have or how strong your vision is, you need abundant leadership capacity to effectively manage, let alone transform, an institution. Trying to be a hero by being a "one-person show" does not work since your success as president will come through the success of your team. Your job is to lead by enabling others.

There are two key dimensions to having an effective executive leadership team. The first is building the team and the second is nurturing the team. They are equally important. Getting the right people on the bus who can add functional *and* strategic skillsets at the executive table is paramount. However, assuming that your role stops at recruitment is a fatal mistake, regardless of how strong and talented the people are. The maxim "You need a championship team and not a team of champions" applies to businesses and academic institutions alike. It is your job to both recruit and coach a championship team.

As a new president, once you have confirmed the structure of your executive team and their portfolios, be intentional in the selection (or retention) of team members by knowing what works for you. Identifying and recruiting your team is probably the most important decision—and often the one most under your control—that you make. Having complementary leadership and management styles around the table creates a diverse and dynamic team to lead the institution. Using management and leadership profiles as part of the candidate assessment when recruiting your team can help determine if someone is a good fit for the role, the rest of the team, and you. Extra diligence at the beginning eliminates problems down the road.

Once your team is in place, you need to actively nurture it. A higher education president's team is unlike any other within the institution because of the significant interdependencies among members. Unlike a dean who may have associate deans who have distinct, and generally non-overlapping, portfolios or provosts who have vice-provosts for defined areas of responsibility, a president's team must work together. There are few issues or opportunities that can be managed within one portfolio alone. This means that the cohesiveness and trust around the table need to be solid. If your team is performing well together, this will be apparent to their teams and, ultimately, to the rest of campus. Academic communities feel anxious if they sense that the executive team is not aligned; therefore, continually investing time and energy to bridge differences and create unity pays significant dividends.

As president, you need to commit to team building, often with the support of a leadership coach to elevate the team's performance and hence their impact on the organization. This will strengthen not only the relationship between the president and individual team members, but also, and importantly, relationships among team members. Your team needs to know that you "have their backs" while being held accountable to deliver. Your efforts build loyalty that will be tested in difficult times. The bottom line is that if your team is not functioning well, you have only yourself to blame. As a leader, your team can be your greatest source of satisfaction and pride or the greatest drain on your energy.

In addition to team building, you also need to invest in individual team members by inspiring, motivating, and challenging them. Providing mentorship, guidance, support, and advice to each person allows them to develop and harness their leadership capacities. This will bring out their best to the benefit of the institution. Some members of your team will be potential successors of yours or will take on a presidential role at another institution. Helping prepare them for further leadership opportunities is one of your responsibilities and an expectation of the board with respect to succession planning.

***

Key Takeaways from Lesson No. 6

Don't fall into the hero complex.

- Recognize that significant leadership capacity is required to effectively manage and transform an institution, and your success will come through the success of your team.
- Build your team by having complementary leadership and management styles around the table to create a diverse and dynamic team to lead your institution.
- Nurture your team to strengthen the relationship and trust among team members and to elevate its performance and impact on the organization.
- Inspire, motivate, and challenge each of your team members by providing mentorship, guidance, support, and advice so they develop and harness their leadership capacities.

Lesson No. 7

Build a healthy organization.

"Culture eats strategy for breakfast."

~Peter Drucker

A PRESIDENT NEEDS A CLEAR AND COMPELLING strategy in order to evolve or transform their institution. The process of developing such a strategy engages stakeholders who share the president's perspectives and ambitions and working together shape a vision that drives decisions and impacts. Although this process holds true for virtually all higher education institutions, culture can differ vastly between organizations. Institutional culture is made up of the traditions, norms, and behaviours within an organization and has a major impact on its ability to drive performance to meet its strategic goals.

Institutional culture is a component of a broader concept of building healthy organizations. In higher education, a healthy organization is one that integrates the well-being of faculty and staff into the institution's strategy through tangible support systems, policies, and practices. The development of a healthy higher education environment is driven by the president, and their commitment will set the tone on how this is received and implemented within the organization.

A healthy organization is the essential foundation of a transformative strategic plan since all stakeholders need to feel committed, engaged, and willing to invest discretionary efforts into the institution's future. In fact, most experts in the field of organizational culture argue that without an effective culture, the probability of implementing a successful strategy is low.

Talking about institutional culture and healthy organizations can be uncomfortable for some presidents. Specifically addressing norms, values, and behaviours can lean into an emotional space that can be perceived as being at odds with an academic culture underpinned by critical thought, open debate, and collegial governance. However, higher education institutions are like most organizations in that they consist of people. And it is a universal truth that people need to feel valued, respected, and recognized for their contributions. Being deliberate about the values that shape the organization is important, and these values need to be reflected and reinforced throughout the institution.

Building a healthy organization starts at the top, and the president needs to both model and lead in showcasing desired behaviours. If progress is to be made and maintained, an accountability framework for leaders within the organization to invest in and improve the culture in their faculties and units is also needed. Employee engagement surveys do not measure organizational health or institutional culture directly, but they do provide important quantitative and qualitative information that can also be helpful. Employee engagement refers to employees' commitment to the organization and the level of discretionary effort they are willing to invest, whereas enablement encompasses employees' perceptions of whether they have the resources and support needed to function in their roles. Having this information measured over time in units and faculties provides rich data that can be used to determine where the organization is healthy or not and whether actions eventually lead to improvement.

During unexpected disruptions or crises, a strong and effective culture serves as a shock absorber. A high level of trust in the institution's leaders, a united campus community, and a belief that stakeholders are respected and valued need to be leveraged by a president to lead and manage during tough times.

In today's globally competitive landscape, a healthy organization can truly make an institution stand out relative to its peers. It can impact who is recruited and who will be retained because they believe in both the strategy and their ability to contribute to its success through a supportive environment.

***

Key Takeaways from Lesson No. 7
Build a healthy organization.

- Drive and commit to an effective work environment by modelling the desired behaviours for a healthy organization.
- Develop an accountability framework for leaders within your organization to invest in and improve the culture in their faculties and units.
- Use a strong institutional culture as a shock absorber during crises by leveraging trust in leadership, a united campus, and a belief by stakeholders that they are valued and respected.
- Differentiate your institution through a strong institutional culture, confidence in the strategy, and an ability of stakeholders to contribute to its success.

LESSON NO. 8

Set the bar high.

"Be a yardstick of quality. Some people aren't used to an environment where excellence is expected."

~STEVE JOBS

ONE OF THE MOST IMPORTANT RESPONSIBILITIES a leader has is to set expectations. This responsibility permeates an organization, ultimately leading to the level of performance achieved by individuals and the institution itself. If expectations are set too low, the organization underachieves relative to its potential. Similarly, setting unrealistically high expectations leads to frustration and burnout.

Most leaders agree that their role is to improve performance by creating a culture of excellence. But how do you translate this aspiration into reality? Just asking individuals to perform at a higher level without clearly demonstrating what is expected and providing the required support will usually fall on deaf ears. Most people "don't know what they don't know."

As a higher education president, you need to role model the expectations you set for others. This is often referred to as the "tone at the top," and it means that words and actions count. A leader who is not deemed credible, yet raises performance expectations, will not succeed. Being authentic and having stakeholders appreciate that you do not expect anything of them that you do not expect from yourself is important. Your authenticity and personal responsibility leads to empowerment, creativity, innovation, and ultimately a collective understanding that "good is not good enough." Many will applaud the challenge if they know what is expected of them and will improve their game in response. Others, even with support, may falter and realize that their fit to the institution's direction and expectations is not ideal. They will need to move on to other opportunities. Both of these outcomes should be expected.

There are many areas within an academic institution where setting the bar high has a direct impact on the institution and its culture. A few are discussed here.

The first area is academic performance. Faculty members' performance in teaching, research, and community engagement has the highest impact on an institution's reputation. Recruiting experienced academics or those with strong potential and supporting them appropriately has long-term consequences for an institution. The process to recruit and hire academic faculty therefore needs to focus on excellence upfront to deliver excellence thereafter, while respecting equity, diversity, and inclusion. Similarly, the bar for evaluation, promotion, and tenure also need to be set high to ensure that overall expectations match the desired institutional trajectory. If these are the goals, a president needs to actively communicate, model, and influence the underlying processes. A challenge can arise when someone does not perform at the level expected and because of structures, such as tenure, not much can be done in the short term. Careful management and a focus on those who are strong contributors are required.

The second area is integrity. As a leader, you set the ethical and integrity bar in your organization. Your values are reflected through your actions and will resonate consciously and subconsciously with your faculty, staff, students, and other stakeholders. Setting high expectations of yourself and those around you models these behaviours to others. And consistently doing what is best for your organization and not for yourself demonstrates selflessness and a lack of personal agendas. During a president's tenure, these values will be tested. The courage to face challenges and make decisions that are not necessarily easy but will define the integrity with which your organization operates is the hallmark of setting the bar high.

***

Key Takeaways from Lesson No. 8

Set the bar high.

- Create a culture of excellence to increase the level of performance of individuals and the institution by demonstrating what is expected and providing the required support.
- Role model expectations by being authentic and not expecting anything of others that you do not expect from yourself.
- Actively communicate, model, and influence the processes for excellence in academic recruitment, evaluation, and promotion that have a long-term impact on your institution.
- Set the ethical and integrity bar high by projecting your values through your actions and consistently doing what is best for your organization.

LESSON NO. 9

Anticipate what you can't predict.

"Wisdom consists of the anticipation of consequences."
~NORMAN COUSINS

ONE OF THE MOST DIFFICULT ASPECTS of any leadership role is understanding cause and effect. This is writ large for higher education presidents given the large and diverse number of issues and stakeholders and thus the possibility of creating unintended consequences when decisions are made or actions taken. It is like pulling on a thread; once you start, you don't always know where it will lead, and everything can potentially unravel.

Unfortunately, higher education presidencies do not come with crystal balls. However, as the leader, you need to be capable of making predictions since one of your primary roles is to anticipate issues and opportunities three or four steps ahead. An issue or opportunity rarely exists in isolation as they are usually tied to others that may be activated or nullified depending on what decisions are made or direction taken.

Predicting future events requires exercising strong judgment and lateral thinking. If not, you can be blindsided and also put your organization at risk. Presidents who have the capacity to anticipate the impact of decisions are deemed savvy. Although being able to anticipate a few steps ahead is an innate ability for some, there are skills that you can develop or refine that will strengthen your prescience.

The most important one is triangulation. Each of your executives is the expert in functional skill and strategic insight in their portfolio. Their role is to bring to the executive table their knowledge and judgment within their portfolio scope. They may also have the ability to determine the influence or impact on other portfolios. However, it is the president's job to triangulate across all portfolios as well as the dynamics internal and external to the institution.

A presidency can be thought of as consisting of two pyramids, one on top of each other—point to point. All the information inside the institution flows up to the top of the lower pyramid, while all the relevant external information flows down the upper pyramid to the president in the middle. Interpreting this intersecting information, sometimes called sense making, ensures that all critical factors and impacts are considered. The president sits at this vantage point where all the relevant information should be visible, and they need to use it to make the best decisions on behalf of the institution.

The second skill is scenario planning. Focusing only on the present, as opposed to critically thinking through "If this, then what?" scenarios, will undoubtedly result in increased risk and lost potential for opportunities. Taking the time to rigorously think through alternatives and checking in with trusted advisors can assist in identifying the best course of action. The selection of trusted advisors should be done carefully. They are usually three or four discrete members of the broader community with diverse backgrounds. They can be a sounding board and provide perspective in a safe environment. They have both your institution's and your interests at heart and are willing to invest their personal capacity to assist you in your leadership journey.

***

Key Takeaways from Lesson No. 9

Anticipate what you can't predict.

- Understand cause and effect so there are no unintended consequences when decisions are made or actions taken.
- Exercise strong judgment and lateral thinking so you are not blindsided or putting your organization at risk.
- Triangulate across all portfolios as well as internal and external dynamics to make the best decisions on behalf of your institution.
- Scenario plan by taking time to rigorously think through alternatives and check in with trusted advisors to assist in identifying the best course of action.

LESSON NO. 10

Know and use your political capital.

"Leadership is influence. That's it—nothing more, nothing less."
~JOHN MAXWELL

HIGHER EDUCATION PRESIDENTS HAVE LITTLE POWER. The nature of collegial governance in a bicameral system does not lend itself to top-down decision making. What makes the role interesting is that rather than being directive, you need to inspire, engage, communicate, cajole, and create incentives in order to have any influence on stakeholders and the organization as a whole. As someone once said, "Being a higher education president is like being in a cemetery . . . lots of bodies under you but nobody's listening."

Some of a leader's ability to influence is related to their position. Just having the title of president does carry weight. However, a much broader and deeper ability to influence is related to their political capital. What is political capital? It's all the components, such as their reputation, credibility, and network, that allow a leader to get a job done.

Political capital must be earned. It is gained through every interaction, decision, and compromise; you build trust as well as comfort with your values and leadership style. It works like a piggy bank. Over time, political capital is accumulated in the piggy bank as a precious resource. In fact, there are many piggy banks since the amount of political capital you have with one person or stakeholder group may differ greatly from another. Building political capital takes time and must be grounded in the development of genuine and authentic relationships. Being transactional in your approach to relationship building may give you a false sense of your political capital.

The real value of political capital is its use. It must be spent to be useful, and it should not be squandered. A higher education president has limited time and capacity to move their organization forward, so they must skillfully use their political capital at the right time to make tough decisions, resolve complex issues, or make key changes. Deploying the right mix of carrots and sticks, while not compromising your basic values, allows you to build bridges and fulfill your vision for the organization while staying true to yourself.

Political capital can also be used to drive opportunities since your voice and opinions may particularly resonate with, and be respected by, strategic stakeholders. You can use your capital to gain traction and benefit for your institution or the broader higher education sector. A president needs to manage upside value and downside risk, and political capital is a necessary ingredient for doing this effectively.

Every time political capital is spent, it must be replenished. The key is knowing how much political capital you have at any time and with whom. Being able to assess, build, and use your political capital relies on strong emotional intelligence. This includes knowing how you are perceived by others and being personally and organizationally aware.

A common mistake many leaders make is assuming they have more political capital than they do. Making difficult decisions when the piggy bank is nearly empty can have significant consequences, especially in a higher education environment that can be unforgiving at times. When you have to make a particularly difficult decision to make, it is helpful to have people in your organization you can trust to let you know how you are perceived and your level of credibility.

Finally, when you take office, there is a honeymoon period that should not be confused with political capital. During this period, which could last three, six, or twelve months, you are often given the benefit of the doubt. You might be able to make tough decisions without significant pushback. However, take care to build the piggy bank of political capital, or stakeholder patience and support may quickly fade.

***

Key Takeaways from Lesson No. 10

Know and use your political capital.

- Earn political capital through every interaction, decision, and compromise, which builds trust as well as comfort with your values and leadership style.
- Spend political capital at the right time to make tough decisions, resolve complex issues, make key changes, or drive important opportunities.
- Know how much political capital you have at any time and with whom by being both personally and organizationally aware.
- Replenish your political capital so that difficult decisions are not made when it's low, which can lead to significant consequences.

Lesson No. 11

Make the tough decisions.

"The most difficult thing is the decision to act, the rest is merely tenacity."

~Amelia Earhart

HIGHER EDUCATION INSTITUTIONS ARE FILLED with processes and committees to ensure that fair and equitable decisions are made on a variety of topics. The engagement that faculty, staff, and students invest in these processes is the foundation of collegial governance; although at times bureaucratic, this foundation has served academic institutions well for generations.

Not all decisions within an academic institution flow through these processes and committees, however. There are many decisions, both large and small, that are made across an institution on a daily basis by people based on their roles and responsibilities. Unfortunately, it is the most difficult and complex issues that land on a president's desk. If a decision was straightforward, someone else in the institution would have made it.

Although making difficult decisions comes with being a higher education president, there will always be a level of discomfort with decisions that have major consequences for people, finances, or institutional reputation. This is to be expected and should compel a president to focus their full attention on the issue at hand. Discomfort should not lead, however, to an inability or an unwillingness to make tough decisions. Nor should it lead to decisions that satisfy a vocal few rather than the institution. Poor decision making can paralyze your team and the institution as a whole.

One reason that leaders shy away from making tough decisions is a fear of failure. As stated previously, decisions have consequences. There may be times when a decision does not turn out well and the president is held accountable. Nevertheless, it could be argued that if no decision is made, then there is also no accountability. Some presidents use this logic to defer (permanently in some cases) decisions to minimize failures. The greater risk, however, is that if decisions are not made, progress is hindered and the seeds of frustration are sown.

Another reason for not making decisions is the risk of being disliked. Some leaders link perceived personal popularity with effective leadership; however, the two are usually not highly correlated. A leader's goal is to be respected. A board does not recruit a president to be merely a "nice" person. They want a respected and respectful leader who can make decisions in the best interests of the institution.

Two important concepts support a leader's ability in making difficult decisions: transparency and consistency. Transparency refers to the way in which decisions are made. It does not mean that all decisions need to be made public since they may be sensitive or confidential. However, it does mean that that a clear process is followed using the right people and assessing the relevant information and circumstances. Once a decision is made, you should be able to clearly explain and defend how and why it was made.

The second concept for supporting difficult decision making is consistency. Making ad hoc or inconsistent decisions will, over time, create anxiety and erode trust with your executive team and potentially beyond. Being consistent not only enhances trust, it also leads to predictability. A high-functioning executive team can predict a president's decision with a high level of probability. The president's values, decision-making thought processes, and record of past decisions all feed into predictability. A strategic plan provides a platform to anchor and guide consistent decision making.

While some presidents may not sufficiently engage in difficult decision making, the other end of the spectrum is presidents who get involved in too many difficult issues. The expression "know what hills to die on" applies to a higher education presidency since you only have so much time, energy, and political capital. Trying to push hard simultaneously on several fronts can lead to chaos. Exercising discipline when determining which issues to take on and which ones are better left for another time (or president) is a skill. And a danger is that once you touch an issue, you tend to own it. It can prove very problematic to delegate it back down through the organization.

Finally, when making decisions, recognize that you will make mistakes. It may be because of a lack of information, changing circumstances, or unintended consequences that were not anticipated. There is no shame in admitting a mistake was made and then changing direction and focusing on a new path. This approach will usually earn you respect in the long term.

***

Key Takeaways from Lesson No. 11

Make the tough decisions.

- Make decisions using a clear process, involving the right people and relevant information, so you can clearly explain and defend how and why the decisions were made.
- Build consistency and predictability in your decision making through your values, thought processes, and record of past decisions.
- Exercise discipline regarding the issues you take on and which ones you leave for another time. Trying to push hard simultaneously on several fronts can lead to chaos.
- Admit when a mistake is made, and then change direction and focus on a new path. This will earn you respect in the long term.

Lesson No. 12

Communicate, communicate, communicate.

"The single biggest problem in communication is the illusion it has taken place."

~George Bernard Shaw

A HIGHER EDUCATION PRESIDENT is their institution's chief storyteller and cheerleader. You are the central hub of information, achievements, and aspirations for the organization, which is a powerful platform from which to educate, inspire, and activate stakeholders. This platform needs to be carefully and intentionally used to further the institution's goals and build a strong and effective culture.

A president is the face of the institution, which means that virtually everything you say and do will be interpreted, rightly or wrongly. Sometimes this can border on the comical, such as when a mere comment or gesture is misconstrued; most often, however, misinterpreted comments or actions can lead to confusion and chaos. A lack of clear and consistent communication amplifies this confusion.

One of the biggest challenges with communication is the sheer number and diversity of stakeholders associated with the institution.

Identifying the right channels and curating the most relevant content to communicate to each stakeholder takes planning, which is where a strong strategic communications team is invaluable. Having communications professionals within the institution map out these channels and content ensures consistency of messaging and an effective use of the president's time. These professionals can also ensure that you are aligned with the brand of your particular institution so that the right image is presented authentically.

One of the most important groups that you need to communicate clearly and consistently with is your executive team. Although this may seem obvious, many leadership teams don't reach their potential because of a lack of shared information, clarity on direction, or timing of decisions. A servant-leader model is centred on the leader who enables and empowers their team by constantly engaging with them, both formally and informally, to ensure that they have the right information at the right time to do their jobs effectively. Formal engagement consists of scheduled group or individual meetings while informal engagement refers to the flow of information through unscheduled meetings, calls, and emails. Teams that are in sync through constant sharing of information will be more effective than those that aren't. And stakeholders will have more confidence in them.

The board also needs consistent communication and information with the president. Information on the institution's strategy, progress, and issues, as well as the broader higher education sector or external environment, helps a board provide advice and oversight. This communication must be ongoing since the environment itself is constantly evolving and also because board membership may turn over relatively rapidly. Consistent communication with your board, board executive, and board chair ensures that you are providing them with the right information at the right time. This particularly applies to issues that undoubtedly will arise on your campus. Board members don't want surprises and will naturally raise concerns when they learn about issues in the media. A clear issues management framework should be developed to notify the board on important issues without bringing them into day-to-day operational issues.

In terms of broader communication to stakeholders, there are three rules of thumb for a president. The first is a focus on inspiration. A president's energy, passion, and positive view of the future must inspire stakeholders. The second is that once is not enough. Key messages need be repeated many times for them to sink in. The third is consistency, in other words having a limited number of messages that are consistently communicated to foster cohesion and alignment.

Internal stakeholders require clear and ongoing communication. The channels to reach faculty, staff, and students can include small group forums, town halls, visits to faculties or labs, or regular walks through campus to have informal chats. It can also include blogs, tweets, or videos depending on a president's personal comfort with, or desire to use, these channels. Whatever means is used, a president must be visibly engaged with their campus community. Stakeholders expect to see and hear from their president, and this role cannot be delegated.

External stakeholders, consisting of alumni, community leaders, donors, government, and the public at large, consider a higher education president as a thought leader with a powerful platform from which to speak on issues. There is interest in your voice and perspectives that are shaped by your having a seat at important tables and a macro view of trends. Using this platform strategically through speeches, opinion editorials, participation on panels, and other forums can position your institution as a leader and build its external reputation.

Communication in a time of crisis can test a president since verbal and non-verbal cues are amplified when dealing with difficult situations. Being calm and in control inspires confidence and reassures the campus community. If a president is unsure or tentative, others can become uneasy and anxious. What starts as a ripple at the presidential level can build into a tsunami throughout a campus.

Communication is not just about talking. It is also about listening. Active listening at the individual and stakeholder levels provides insight that can be used to check assumptions. One of the most important aspects of leadership is the ability to understand other peoples' motivations, which may not be the same as your own. These motivations drive behaviours that may appear contrary to how you would behave but are consistent with their motivational values. For

example, if you are driven by performance and someone else by relationships or process, you will approach issues differently. This different approach can bring about friction or conflict. Understanding "why" someone behaves in a certain way is as important as "what" they do.

Investing time and energy into honing communication skills, including dealing with media, can serve a president well in both the good times and the tough times and will pay significant dividends in supporting their leadership effectiveness.

***

Key Takeaways from Lesson No. 12

Communicate, communicate, communicate.

- Leverage your platform as chief storyteller and cheerleader to educate, inspire, and galvanize stakeholders.
- Use a servant-leader model to enable and empower your team through formal and informal communication so they have the right information to do their jobs effectively.
- Communicate with internal and external stakeholders by harnessing your energy and passion and by iterating a few key messages that bring cohesion and alignment.
- Invest time and energy into honing your communication skills, including dealing with media; this will pay significant dividends in good times and in tough times.

Lesson No. 13

Expect a crisis so prepare for one.

"Leaders play a unique role in periods of crisis and chaos. Because if you don't, you're not going to harness the power of all the people behind you."

~Lynn Good

THERE WILL BE DAYS WHEN A WELL-PLANNED SCHEDULE goes off the rails. A crisis emerges from left field, and it will be all consuming to you and your team, and perhaps even your board. Crises are more than the issues that typically impact higher education institutions, such as a faculty member who may have said something controversial and has riled up stakeholders, or students who are displeased with a decision made by administration. Although these situations can lead to a crisis, they can usually be taken care of with a strong issues management framework and a proactive leadership team. Be vigilant about differentiating issues from crises since you can "create your own weather" if you overreact to an issue.

A crisis is a seminal event that can have devastating impact on faculty, staff, or student health and safety; the environment; the institution's finances; or infrastructure. And in all cases, a crisis has the potential to have significant effects on the institution's—and the president's—reputation. Given the long lifespan of an academic institution, its reputation will eventually recover from a negative impact. However, a president's reputation may not; therefore, a crisis carries significant personal risk.

There are four steps a president can take to *prepare* for a crisis. The first step is to provide leadership and oversight to the institution's emergency response plan (ERP). A plan must be in place before a crisis occurs because trying to figure your plan out while a crisis is unfolding leads to chaos. The development of an ERP that has a clearly defined structure is critical. Clearly articulate the membership of the crisis management team, which makes strategic decisions, and the emergency operations group, which develops and leads operational decisions, so that leaders can assume their expected roles as soon as the crisis develops. The plan should consist of a comprehensive and integrated emergency management and business continuity program linked to enterprise risk management, health and safety, and other programs. It should also encompass a crisis communication plan that describes procedures and actions required to communicate to the higher education community and public, thus assisting in protecting and enhancing the institution's reputation. Ongoing preparation and improvement should also be done through crisis management tabletop exercises, which simulate crisis situations. It should be stressed that an emergency response plan will only be successful with presidential and executive leadership support and engagement.

The second step is to ensure policies and processes are up to date as these will be tested in a crisis. A third step is to learn from past crises elsewhere. Many higher education institutions that have experienced a crisis have reports or recommendations from which you can learn. A final step is to build strong one-on-one community relationships. Existing relationships with the chief of police and mayor, as examples, are important since you may need to quickly draw on these people in a crisis.

Once a crisis develops, there are four key elements to *lead* in a crisis. The first element is to define the objectives of the response. These are the guiding principles that should drive strategic and operational decision making. As an example from a real crisis resulting in the tragic loss of life of several students in an off-campus incident, the objectives could be to (1) demonstrate care and concern to those affected; (2) effectively direct members of the higher education community to support services and answer their questions in a timely manner; (3) ensure students are not negatively impacted in their academic studies; (4) ensure all messaging is accurate, sensitive, and timely; and (5) provide appropriate venues for people to express themselves, share their condolences, and receive support from one another.

The second element is to be clear as to your role as president during a crisis. By remaining at the strategic and reputational level, you let your team do the jobs for which they are trained. The true test of leadership is how you respond in a crisis when you need to harness your sense of calm, your creative energies, and your solution-oriented approach. Seeking advice from colleagues who lead institutions that have gone through crises can provide a safe space for dialogue and support.

The third element is recognition that the first 24 hours wins. Perceptions solidify quickly in a crisis, and given the widespread use of social media, there is a high probability that misinformation will circulate. Being able to have accurate information communicated in a timely matter can have a tremendous impact on reputation.

The final element is to debrief and learn. Every crisis is different, but learnings can be developed and used for ongoing improvement. Using a rigorous process to assess the strengths and weaknesses of the response ensures that changes are discussed and documented for the next time.

Crises impacting a higher education institution can have a significant impact beyond the event itself. If managed and led effectively, they can result in a stronger and more resilient community and even a heightened reputation for the institution.

***

Key Takeaways from Lesson No. 13

Expect a crisis so prepare for one.

- Differentiate issues from crises so you don't "create your own weather" by overreacting to an issue.
- Prepare for a crisis by having an emergency response plan before a crisis occurs so you are not figuring your plan out while a crisis is unfolding, which leads to chaos.
- Lead in a crisis by staying at the strategic and reputational levels and harnessing your sense of calm and your solution-oriented approach.
- Debrief and learn from each crisis using a rigorous process to assess the strengths and weaknesses of the response so that changes are documented for the future.

Lesson No. 14

Embrace governance as your friend.

"Organizations with good governance practices in place can be shown to be more successful than organizations without."

~Alison Holt

HIGHER EDUCATION INSTITUTIONS ARE UNIQUE in terms of their governance systems. The terms "bicameral" governance and "collegial" governance not only relate to the specific structures for oversight and decision making, they also describe a culture of participation and transparency that underpins a strong governance framework.

Governance matters on higher education campuses—a lot. Its importance is increasing, with organizations being held to a high standard of oversight by their academic senates and boards and greater accountability from both internal and external stakeholders. Whether it is the public, government, donors, students, or faculty, there is an expectation that higher education institutions are using their resources wisely and making decisions in the best long-term interests of the institution on behalf of the communities they serve.

A president has a direct impact on the quality of governance at their institution. The time, energy, interest, and support you personally invest will be apparent to your team, governance bodies, and other stakeholders inside and outside your organization. Being prepared and actively participating in meetings tangibly demonstrate your commitment. Good governance protects you and the organization.

Effective governance starts with structures, practices, and policies that are up to date and benchmarked against high-performing, well-run organizations inside and outside the higher education sector. Regular reviews of governing documents, policies, and processes ensure that they are current and effective. It is particularly important to clarify the role of the board and board members in the governance system and in relation to other participants in this system, and also in areas such as fundraising and government relations. Board members also need to be educated about conflict of interests so there is no risk of confusion. Finally, annual board evaluations should be conducted for feedback and commitment to ongoing improvement.

Good governance is also required to support a high-functioning academic senate. Similar to the board, the senate requires clear mandates and terms of reference for their committees, as well as annual work plans and senate evaluations. This will ensure that senators understand the functioning of collegial governance and that they remain engaged. All of these efforts can be supported by an effective and experienced governance secretary who is the governance expert on campus and whose role and impact is increasing within the higher education sector.

A higher education board has oversight in four key areas: strategy, risk, stewardship of financial resources, and assurance that the mandate is being met. For many people, a strategy or vision is an esoteric concept and needs to be brought to ground level to be understood. This is especially difficult for board members as many do not live day to day within the organization. A president must draw clear linkages between the strategy and initiatives, investments, outcomes, and impacts so the board can clearly see and oversee how the strategy is being implemented. You are at significant risk if your board does not understand the institution's strategic direction and progress on goals. Regular reporting on progress using dashboards and Key Performance Indicators should be done. The board's oversight responsibility is met through their oversight of the president (and through the president, other key leaders), so a strong performance planning framework should be in place that links your annual goals to actions, metrics/deliverables, and results.

Governance provides the framework for president–board relations. Using your board (usually through the executive committee if you have one) to discuss and seek feedback on key developments or issues at an early stage ensures that you don't make major decisions without their knowledge, input, and support. Examples of major decisions include large donations with potential reputational impacts, significant issues with stakeholder groups, or contemplated changes in your executive team.

Recognize that reporting to a board is different than reporting to an individual, and some presidents find this dynamic challenging to understand and manage. Although the board chair normally has the closest relationship with, and highest impact on, a president, other board members may have significant influence at the board table or on the board chair. In addition, many of the members of the board will not be from the higher education sector, and virtually none will have served as a higher education president. Some will be representatives of particular constituencies, such as students, faculty, or staff, and may have difficulty separating their responsibility as a board member from their responsibilities to their constituencies or interests. Deep knowledge of your role, as well as the risks and complexities of your job, will be limited, and this creates risk for you when you and your board are misaligned. Steady and ongoing two-way communication with the board allows you to monitor signals of potential misalignment so that they can be dealt with accordingly; if not done, your board may be one of your highest risks. As the saying goes, "Boards love you until they don't."

Another challenge for a president is that there will be regular turnover in board chairs and members during their term. Depending on the institution's charter or legislation, there may be a significant number of people who flow through the board. Careful onboarding of members and skillful management by the chair will enhance members' abilities to contribute at the board table. It can be anticipated that the people who were involved in your selection as president will not be the same people around the table three, five, or seven years out. This means that you need to continually nurture and develop your relationship with board members.

Finally, service on a higher education board is different than in the corporate sector. The nature and dynamics of a higher education institution with its multiplicity of vocal stakeholders can have a significant impact on board decisions, particularly those involving the president. For example, if significant numbers of students, faculty members, or government officials express an overwhelming lack of confidence in a president, a board may be compelled to act even if they believe the president is doing a good job.

Invest your time and energy in a strong governance system. This will provide you with support, clear and accountable decision-making processes, and sometimes, political cover.

***

Key Takeaways from Lesson No. 14

Embrace governance as your friend.

- Invest your personal time and support to ensure good governance through clear and accountable decision-making processes. This will protect both you and your organization.
- Ensure effective governance is grounded in structures, practices, and policies that are up to date and benchmarked against high-performing, well-run organizations.
- Practise ongoing two-way communication with your board to monitor signals of potential misalignment so they can be dealt with in a timely manner and to mitigate risk.
- Conduct annual board and academic senate evaluations to gather feedback and demonstrate a commitment to ongoing improvement.

Lesson No. 15

Enjoy the ride!

"It is fun to have fun but you need to know how."

~Dr. Seuss

IT IS A PRIVILEGE TO SERVE AS A HIGHER EDUCATION president. Being the steward of an institution that forms such an important part of the fabric of its communities is both a tremendous opportunity and responsibility. It is also a unique experience, the more so as there are a limited number of higher education presidents. This means that direct knowledge of the complexity and joy of leading a higher education institution is known to relatively few.

Although a presidency has its good days and tough days, the good will undoubtedly outnumber the bad. The key is to nurture and enjoy the experience by learning and growing while having some fun along the way. The relationships developed and the potential to create a profound impact are the rewards.

Since every higher education presidency is unique, each president needs to develop a model that works for them in order to truly enjoy the role while being effective. However, there are a few guiding principles that can assist in making the most of the experience.

The first is to have patience. This is one of the toughest challenges for many leaders. People take on leadership roles to drive change and make a difference, ambitions that are not usually compatible with patience. If you are not careful, the work can become frenetic and chaotic, rather than planned and purposeful.

Exercising patience is really about managing expectations, that is, managing the expectations that others have of you, and perhaps more often, the expectations that you have of yourself. Striving for clarity in strategy, plans, and outcomes allows you to maintain focus and ensures that expectations with all stakeholders are clear.

The second guiding principle is not getting caught up in the daily setbacks or challenges. This means learning to filter out the "noise" and celebrating small successes along the way. Organizational change and overall success is not measured in days or weeks, but rather months and years. Your role is to focus on the long-term goals.

The third guiding principle is ensuring that you have time for yourself beyond the role of higher education president. Always being "on" can be both tiring and stressful, so spending time on hobbies and fitness and with family and friends can provide balance and perspective. Building in downtime, such as using air travel to think and rest rather than packing in more work, will ultimately benefit you and your organization. And using your vacation not only allows you to refresh and recharge, it also models to your team that time away is important.

And perhaps most importantly to remember is why we do what we do. In the case of a higher education president it is very simple: we want to ensure that our students have a great educational experience and our research has positive impacts on society and its quality of life. Being able to champion the importance of higher education falls on the shoulders of higher education presidents. If you are not articulating the value of higher education, who else will?

When the job appears daunting, remember that there is a high level of respect and admiration—albeit often from the silent majority—for taking on a higher education presidency. Investing in your leadership capacity to strengthen your impact will serve both you and your community in carrying out this important role.

Enjoy the ride!

***

Key Takeaways from Lesson No. 15

Enjoy the ride!

- Develop a model as president that works for you so you can truly enjoy the experience while being effective.
- Exercise patience by managing the expectations that others have of you and you have of yourself by striving for clarity in strategy, plans, and outcomes.
- Filter out the "noise" and celebrate small successes along the way since organizational change and overall success is measured in months and years, not days or weeks.
- Take time for yourself beyond the role of president by spending time on hobbies and fitness and with family and friends to provide balance and perspective.

About the Author

Dr. Elizabeth Cannon, OC, is president emerita of the University of Calgary after serving as its president and vice chancellor from 2010 to 2018. A champion for advancing the mission of the university and fostering excellence in higher education, she led the development of the university's transformational *Eyes High* strategy and its $1.3 billion *Energize* campaign through a focus on impact and a strong institutional culture. Before her presidency, she was dean of the Schulich School of Engineering at the University of Calgary.

Elizabeth is an internationally recognized researcher of Global Positioning Systems (GPS) in both industrial and academic environments and has commercialized technology for more than 200 agencies worldwide. Currently, she is a speaker on leadership, strategy, and innovation, as well as co-author of the upcoming book *Strategic University Management: Future Proofing Your Institution*. She is an active seed-stage investor and mentor, particularly for female-founded companies, and serves on numerous non-profit and corporate boards. Elizabeth has received more than 50 teaching, research, and leadership awards, including being selected as one of *Canada's Top 100 Most Powerful Women*, receiving five honorary degrees, and being named an Officer of the Order of Canada.

Made in the USA
Monee, IL
25 August 2020

39766353R00046